Don't Marry A Lemon!

A Marriage Therapist's Advice on
Choosing the Right Mate the First Time

By Brett J. Novick, LMFT

TRAIN OF THOUGHT

PRESS

Publisher's Note

This book is designed to provide information and motivation to our readers. It is sold with the understanding that the publisher is not engaged to render any type of psychological, legal, or any other kind of professional advice. No warranties or guarantees are expressed or implied by the publisher's choice to include any of the content in this volume. Neither the publisher nor the individual author shall be liable for any physical, psychological, emotional, financial, or commercial damages, including, but not limited to, special, incidental, consequential, or other damages. Our views and rights are the same: You are responsible for your own choices, actions, and results.

ISBN: 978-0-9861485-6-9
Library of Congress: 2017949019
TOTPID: 08312017BNMAL

Summary: Marriage therapist gives advice on how to choose the right partner for marriage

Connie Johnston
Train of Thought Press
2275 Huntington Drive, #306
San Marino, CA 91108
www.TrainOfThoughtPress.com

TRAIN OF THOUGHT
PRESS

Dedication

"I'm lucky in having found the perfect partner
to spend my life with."

-- Sara Paretsky

To my wonderful wife, Darla who taught me the meaning of marriage and relationships. You are my inspiration and inspire me to be a better man, husband and father.

To my late father, Dr. William Novick, thank you for teaching me how to be a husband and father. You were a wonderful mentor and I could not have asked for more.

To my mother, Georgine Davis, thank you for always teaching me to do the right thing.

To Billy and Sami, you both are my pride and joy. I hope that the years ahead provide you back the wonderful and happy memories you provide me each day.

This book, is most of all dedicated to you- the reader. It is my hope that I can give you what I have learned about relationships as a marriage and family therapist, a husband, a friend, and a father. I hope that you find what it is that you are looking for is found, at least partially, in these pages.

Table of Contents

Introduction...
Why This Book?

"I've got a new relationship and I'm trapped in this old life."
-- Moon Unit Zappa

When my wife and I were dating, we had seen a poster of a H. Jackson Brown Jr. quote that has always stuck with me, "Choose your life's mate carefully from this one decision will come 90% of your happiness...or misery." Unfortunately, I have seen all too many of those, whose 90% has been on the opposing side of that balance. In turn, those couples have lived lives of sadness in which home is a prison, work, drinking or drugs are an escape and have children left scraping by on the remaining ten percent.

It is so easy to get into a relationship and quickly develop buyer's remorse. In my time as a family therapist, I have seen so many people settle for relationships and then realize a year or two down the line that they are left with a lemon. Worse yet, is when children are entered into the mix, or people continue to drive relationships that are unhealthy, unable to be repaired, or even dangerous with children unrestrained in the backseat in tow.

When someone is drowning and desperate, they will grab on to whoever will keep them afloat for the next breath of air. In fact, as a trained lifeguard, we were always told to be very cautious around these people in distress because they will drown both rescuer and themselves in a frantic effort to simply breathe. So, it is with

1

relationships, if one cannot find the "right guy" we reach out to the "guy right now" and hope that they will be the life preserver that leads us through the waves of trials and tribulations that couples must sustain to succeed. Unfortunately, many times we drown in a sea of good intentions.

In my two decades as a marriage and family therapist, over and over, I see relationships when they are already in a dangerous tailspin that gets increasingly difficult to pull out of. When we dissect the partnerships, we find the origins of the relationship were fraught with many cracks in the foundation. Ultimately, as the relationship grew, so did those cracks, and ultimately the couple crumbled.

Often times with relationships we use terms like, "it was fate…I am looking for my soulmate…I will just know when it is right." Therefore, we place this important decision solely on loose hopes and romantic aspirations. Please know, these qualities do have an important aspect in all relationships, however, we also must use a skeptical eye. When we place more consumer discretion on deciding the type of latte, apartment, or car we want for the moment, than on a lifetime relationship, that may be problematic in the long haul of a marriage or union.

There may be many reasons for this. First, when we make a large purchase, we do have some level of emotional involvement. Moreover, we also should have a large degree of consumer skepticism and education on what we are buying. One would hope that they are making a rational, well-informed purchase. We also are concretely aware of how much financial investment we are making in this very costly decision.

In relationships, our ability to use such practicality can quickly go out the window. Emotionality fogs our ability to think with a rational and clear mind and so we are left reacting primarily through feeling. Feelings are not logical, and logic is devoid of feelings causing love and logic lines to sometimes blur. When these two do, we then attempt to rationalize, minimize, or legitimize how we have come to this place in which our relationship has reached a crossroads of potential demise.

What we will discuss here is how to take some of the emotion out of the relational decision-making. Then when it is right, romance, love, warmth, and all of these things that are vital will flow in naturally. Only then, can you seriously consider someone to occupy the most sacred and precious part of your life and heart with.

In this book, we are going to look at the other side, what is "under the hood" of the person, you may want to join in relationship with. I have seen far too many relationships evaporate when one of the partners realized they looked at the body of the car, and when they gazed under the hood it was a mess, had parts missing, or they were not able to fix or change the critical flaws.

We are going to look under the hood of relationships so we know what we are observing. There are no emotions, it is a job, and we should be somewhat competent in getting the four wheels back on the relational road.

We will meet many salesmen in our relationship journey, who take a different tact, those who operate and play on your emotions. When you open the door to the car dealership of relationships and the automated bell dings, it is the beginning of the first round of a fight.

A fight for you to leave with a vehicle and without your money (or in the case of relations that of your emotional investment). The salesperson who is savvy operates on the emotional components of your psyche. They want to sell an image to you of what life will be with the car that you are going to be leaving with. The salesperson does not want you to walk out the door without a sale and they will play on your feelings and trust to facilitate this.

Unfortunately, if you leave steered by emotions alone, you may be asking yourself, "What did I just do? How was I able to be convinced to purchase that car? With those extras?" As the buyer's remorse sets in, you may ask yourself, "How was I so easily convinced? What did I not see?"

I am writing this book, for a number of reasons. I am writing this book as though you were a member of my family. As the older brother to two sisters, as a friend, as a marriage and family therapist, and (most importantly) as the father to a daughter who I hope will find someone that she could share her life with fully.

Often, I joke with my daughter "she is not going to date until she is married." Of course, I say this in jest, and know she must explore, make mistakes, and learn what it is she is looking for. I write this book for her and, dear reader, for you. On these pages, I am putting writing what I have learned about relationships in my life as a marriage and family therapist, a husband, a father and a friend.

Now, let's take a look at the car lot of the partnerships of life. Let us kick the tires, look under the hood, read up and make an educated choice. Your 90% awaits…

Lesson 1: Don't Settle... This Is A Big Purchase- Get What You Want or Save Up for It

"There is no passion to be found playing small - in settling for a life that is less than the one you are capable of living."
-- Nelson Mandela

"Where do you want to go for dinner?" It is a question that is batted around by many couples, friends, and families around the country. We think, "Do I want pizza, Italian, Chinese, burgers, or something else?" In the end, you may say, "I don't care...whatever you want."

Then the group or person you are with decided emphatically, "Let's get pizza!" Now, you are relieved that a choice was made, but then you realize "I really wanted a burger tonight."

You say nothing, you said you did not care, and so you settle in half-heartedly for another night of pizza. However, let us imagine it was a larger purchase; like your dream car? Would you be just as likely to settle in and allow the chips to fall where they may? I would hope not, the stakes are much higher. Let's suppose in this chapter we were in the market for your first (or your dream) car.

So it is time: you have been waiting and saving a lifetime for your dream car. You skimp and save for a shot to get what you want. As you walk into the car lot you can hear your heart beat in your ears, feel the cold sweat of excitement, and the clamminess of your cold palms. You look around and scan vehicles for as far as the eye can see. New and old cars, vehicles of every type, size, age, and condition.

It is overwhelming. How do you make a choice? You know you want the best car for you. However, what kind? What color? How do you purchase the best one for the money? As these thoughts swirl around your head creating a murky snow globe of feelings, the dealer approaches you. He can sense a customer who is overwhelmed and confused. Like a shark, he smells blood in the water and quickly moves in for the financial kill.

"How can I help you? "The question is asked in a manner that seems more a sly statement than an actual inquiry. You are thrusted back into the reality of the moment and stammer, "Uh, I don't really know what I want. I have been dreaming about getting a sports car...I am just really not sure what kind. I just know that I have been saving for years and know I have really wanted one for as long as I could remember."

"No problem," he chuckles. "Give me half the deposit and I will give you this key... It will start one of the cars here in the lot." You think for a moment, impulsivity gets the best of you and you whip out the never used checkbook for the account saved just for this purpose. "How much do I owe you?"

You are quick to write out the check as your hands tremble with excitement. You daydream of driving your new car, the sun on your face, the wind flowing in your hair, and becoming the envy of all your friends.

He hands you the key, which gleams like a diamond. You scratch your head and ask, "Where's the car?" The dealer dryly replies, "I dunno..." You follow up with, "What kind of car is it?" The dealer returns a blank stare and shrugs his shoulders. "What color... what year... what model?"

The dealer hurriedly puts your check in his shirt pocket and staggers away; disappearing into the horizon of vehicles. Now excitement flashes into an inferno of panic and rage. The only thing you have left is a key and several thousands of dollars less to your name.

In desperation, you grip the key in your hand and begin systematically opening each car. Old ones and new ones, compacts, and SUVs, exotics and domestics, colors of every kind, cars of every shape and size.

No longer is the importance of the dream you had. Now, your short-term goal is simply a vehicle that works and can drive you home from this sea of metal and rubber. As you grow in desperation, you jam the key into each ignition. Convincing yourself that perhaps shoving the key in harder, twisting and turning faster, will somehow force the engine to turn over and work. Your only hope now is to hear the purr of an engine; any engine.

Don't Settle:

You may say that this scenario is crazy, unrealistic, or impossible. Maybe it seems like a bizarre dream of someone who ate too much spicy food before retiring to a fitful sleep.

Yet, how many of us settle regarding something far more valuable and vital then a car... that of our potential intimate relationships?

7

Often, we have dreams of a lifetime partner that develops over years of plans and hopes. We take these wishes and then blindly try to fit the key of our heart into a partnership that may run smoothly and travel down the road of life. Despite our best wishes, we find the key does not fit or the car stalls only a short time down the relational road.

So many of those that I have seen as a marriage and family therapist over my nearly two decades of counseling people and in watching friends, peers, and colleagues have parallel life experiences such as these. I have found all too many partners are ready to throw up their hands and settle for a bond that is so much less than ideal.

My first relationship suggestion in making a good consumer choice is simple, and yet exceedingly difficult, don't settle. Many of us are more likely to research our next car or smartphone then our next or current relationship.

Let's look at what are the introduction to the basics to avoid settling in the relationship arena.

The types of vehicles in the car lot are plentiful and diverse…Let's meet them briefly before we take them for a test drive:

This Book Is Applicable for Any Kind of Vehicle You May Be Looking for:

In that car lot of life there is a host of potential vehicles, types, colors, ages, and styles. Think about the number of vehicles you can name and then think further of the exponential sum of types and features each car can possibly have. This is a parallel with the variety of connections we potentially can, and do, foster with others in our lives; it is almost limitless.

In the diverse, and ever flattening world, we reside in relationships are as varied as the mosaic of persons on the globe that we are blessed to live upon. Traditional, same sex, multiracial, interfaith, intercultural, and a host of other partnerships are being developed as we all become increasingly accepting of each other. In understanding these diversities, we recognize how much we are more the same, than differ, from those we inhabit the world with those around us.

I tell you this, because I want you to understand that in my years of counseling all types of people, couples, and families, the needs, concerns, and subjects covered in this book are useful for any relationship. As you counsel a host of different cross-sections of people, you quickly realize that although the faces are varied the issues are much more similar then dissimilar; relationships need the same soil to take root and grow.

True, all couples face some idiosyncratic differences. This being said, however, each partnership can learn something from our time together in this book.

A Compact Car Cannot Become a Sports Model nor Vice Versa:

Many of us enter relationships with the hope of "changing" our partner. It could be the way they act, treat others, dress, eat, hygiene, etc. The belief is that if you try hard enough, do an ample amount of nagging, or are have an ample amount of patience your partner will change because of sheer willpower or because they love you.

First off, if your loved one has developed a particular habit, it likely has become engrained over years (or decades). Therefore, it becomes difficult to even recognize the habits you want to have changed by the person as they have become automatic in nature. According to Gretchin Rubin, Author of The Happiness Project [1] it "took an average of sixty-six days" to change a habit. Can you, therefore, keep up your nagging for over two months daily without driving both of you crazy?

Sure, you can make some changes within a limited range. It is akin to putting some sporty looking flames and a spoiler on the back of a compact vehicle. Point is, it is still a compact not the sports car (no matter what you call it). People are only capable of making changes if they are aware of what they are doing and most of what we do, in terms of habits, are done without much consciousness of what we are doing.

Change is hard and often very uncomfortable. Try remembering to do anything for 66 days straight and you begin to recognize the challenge of change. Focusing on acceptance and realizing that you are seeking a partner with flaws you can live with, versus perfection is a key to successfully driving down the long highway of life.

Rubin, Gretchen. *The happiness project: or, why I spent a year trying to sing in the morning, clean my closets, fight right, read Aristotle, and generally have more fun.* New York: Harper Collins, 2015. Print.

Do You Really Want a Sports Car or Something That Is More Reliable?

Many people are attracted to the outward look of a person. If they are physically attractive, are a challenge that you want to pursue, or someone that is extroverted and portends an outward outgoing personality, they are immediately on your dating radar screen.

These "sporty" personalities sometimes blind us into looking any further into what is on the inside of the person. It is akin to viewing the image of what a sports car looks like, what your friends will think, and how cool you will appear zipping down the street. Simultaneously, with this vision in your head, you ignore any other aspect that you may need to know about the vehicle (i.e. reliability, cost, reputation, if it had been in accident, etc.).

Ask yourself; however, how long will this "sportiness" last? After several years that vehicle will look dinged and beat up, the sportiness will grow tiring as you continue have to put in more gas to keep it's inefficient engine running. In short, it looked good when you bought it, but it is no longer practical when you realize the cost and that a good-ole reliable mini-van may be the best for growing and raising a family.

Additionally, it is no longer the new model. The previous state of the art features are now outdated. That sleek new body type that drew you initially to this sporty car is now long past, as they have created many newer models and sportier body styles.

Too Much Baggage in The Trunk Weighs a Car Down:

When you buy a car, you expect the trunk to be empty, right? In fact, if you purchased a sedan with a lot to weigh it down it would also effect the performance of the car, the ability for it drive, and even the gas mileage to go on your next road trip.

So it is with relationships…you expect to, hopefully, come into a relationship with as little baggage as possible. Do not get me wrong, everyone has something in their "trunk" of baggage. Some have more, some less, some trunks are dirtier then others and others have much more luggage than some.

The issue with too much baggage in one's imagined trunk, is that it impacts the prospective person from truly giving all of themselves in a relationship. On the outset, each party expects as close to 100% of the other as possible. A sports car, nor a relationship, cannot be at its peak performance if weighed down with too many other issues.

Those That Don't Want to Buy the Mini-Van Will Have No Room for Other Passengers:

People joke about a mini-van being the notorious death knell from one's younger and hip lifestyle to the conversion of midlife. It is the reputed entrance from one's identity as a fledgling grown-up to an actual adult and the first stage pervious to the midlife crisis.

Not everyone wants, or is ready, for the commitment of having children. If one partner sees this within their purview on their road of life and the other does not see it anywhere on the horizon that is a definite issue. Yes, you can develop a relationship, but you will always be looking out the rear-view mirror wondering, "What if?"

Your relational tank will never be full and, in turn, your relationship will never be totally fulfilling.

The Vehicle with Faulty Brakes:

Now I know what you are thinking, I would never buy a car with no brakes, right? That would be crazy…it is a recipe for disaster. As you drive, you are constantly aware that those brakes may fail when you need them most. Every turn you are literally taking your life into your own hands and anticipation and worry surround each move you make.

Yet, some of us crave relationships like this. We look for partnerships that have challenge and spontaneity. There always needs to be some new situation that adds abundant positive or negative energy to the relationship. A cycle that is followed by a time of "making up." The issue that occurs, hence, "recharges" the volatile relational battery.

The payoff? Fuel that ignites a relationship and "burns white hot." The problem is that relationships such as these quickly go through the gasoline that enflames the rapport and, sooner than later, burns itself out. High levels of relationships based solely, or majorly, on passion or drama can only last so long before boredom arises, as both partners cannot keep up this exhausting standard for their connection. Put another way, it is not the flames that shoot into the sky that are hottest; it is the glowing embers that glow and smolder at the center of the fire that are the hottest and last to extinguish.

Additionally, and even more concerning, these impulsive relationships often can be tinged with higher level of domestic violence, emotional mistreatment, or illicit substance abuse to fan the flames.

The Vehicle That Does Not Have a Working Gas Pedal:

If you have a vehicle that has no gas pedal, you will certainly be safe. Why? Because you won't get anywhere. What you will get is frustrated in not reaching the goals that you have for your life.

Some people are like this in relationships. They simply cannot get the foot on the gas to make a decision. They are decisively indecisive, and cannot make a decision to commit in a relationship. You may say well he/she is worth the wait. Maybe…but how long is the wait worth? A year, two years, a lifetime? (We will have a discussion more about this later as well).

The Vehicle That Has No Heat:

If a car has no heat, you will have a very uncomfortable drive on the coldest of days. In relationships, you find yourself working as hard as possible, and give 110% of the warmth in the partnership, with nothing in return. You cannot always work harder than your partner, or you will burn out of the partnership.

Relationships are a constant see-saw. At times, you will need to devote more time, and at other times, your partner will need to make that investment to balance the relational homeostasis necessary to balance and recharge the coupling you both have.

Some partners simply will not (or cannot) give you what you need. They will not provide you the warmth in the relationship you seek.

You may pursue them and they may retreat, or just stand still, not giving the emotional return or validation that is important to you.

You, in turn, pursue them waiting on every word or emotional carrot that they dangle in front of you. This is no way to pursue a relationship like this. Doing so, will leave you exhausted and devoid of anything else for others. If someone cannot share emotionally with you, the warmth of the relationship will quickly grow frigid and uncomfortable (no matter how you "good" you think you look in the automobile).

The "Dummy" Lights:

Recently, I was driving my car and the "check engine" light came on. I panicked, after all, I don't know how much a new engine could be...but it has to be a lot of money, right? I checked obsessively through the car manual to see what this could be.

The manual was of little help, as it indicated that the warning light could be a number of potential issues from minor to major. I scoured the internet that revealed the same thing, talked to my son whose hobby is fixing cars, same answer. The answer was, there was no answer, without exploring the issue further and more in depth.

When I got to the mechanic, he explained that these are called "dummy" lights. They are for "dummies" like me that indicate only a potential warning of what could be wrong. In relationships, there are "dummy" lights too. These are warnings that may glare, beep, or otherwise alert us, that some of us ignore.

Some of us enter relationships with sweaty palms, listening for every potential indication that something could go wrong. Others drive along and despite every light beeping, chirping, flashing and screaming we continue to ignore them until we are driving with little more than bald tires and a steering wheel.

We will look at some of these warning signs that, though maybe not specifically detrimental in a relationship, when grouped together may be indicative of a larger concern that you may not have been aware of or have previously ignored.

The Car with No GPS:

If you are going to develop a partnership, you need to know where you are going. If neither partner knows what direction, the relationship is travelling in; you will have a good time, but go nowhere fast.

Just as we have individual goals for ourselves, a relationship is a living system onto its own with objectives, wishes, and desires of how you both are going to trudge through the tumultuous roads of life. The hope? To get to a place where you are both better for the wear and are synergistically a stronger unit then you were as separate entities.

Some people simply do not have the internal GPS of knowing what they want and where they desire to go. In turn, they are infinitely stalled, and the lifestyle a couple adopts, is one in which they remain safely where they are. This may be fine initially, but as you grow into a family, it becomes difficult to adapt to what is needed for the metamorphosis and changes necessary to accommodate that relational growth if you don't know what direction to move towards.

It may be a comfortable relationship, however, comfort does not always equate to satisfaction or fulfillment for either, or both, members of the group.

Watch How the Car Salesman Treats the Valet:

We all have a tendency to be on our very best behavior when we meet someone and begin the process of dating. If we did not, we risk losing that person's partnership before it has even begun. So it is, that you do not see the annoying habits, the sloppiness, or how the person looks when they have the stomach flu or a bad cold. Those negative experiences are placed behind a barrier and locked away until you know the person over a longer period and trust is more firmly established.

The same can be said about the car salesperson. He is trying to put his best foot forward. If he cannot build some modicum of trust with you, you are highly unlikely to make the sizeable purchase of a car. It is a business interaction, but one that involves a charismatic bonding (even if it is short) between you both.

Watch carefully though, if he/she is talking to those that are "under" them (defined as those that cannot do anything to improve their well-being financially, socially, or vocationally). How do they treat the key valet? If they smile and are "nicety nice" to you and then turn to the receptionist to bark out commands that is likely a more accurate accounting of their personality. Parallel this with dating (more on this later). In any case, one must look beyond what is immediately in front of them to gain a grasp as to what the future of a spouse might be.

The Other Reviews of the Car:

When I was younger, my father (an engineer) used to be very careful before he purchased a car. He would spend countless hours poring over reviews of the prospective cars he was interested in potentially purchasing. He would read magazines, ask people, and look at the cars in the dealership from afar.

In short, he was prepared with as much of an unbiased, rational, and non-emotional view of the potential purchase. Knowing that he was going to be keeping the car for the next several years of his life, and literally putting his family's safety in the hands of a car that would take his most precious commodity along the harrowing roads of life.

When we are seeking a relationship, we do not tend to look at the reviews of others or take them as seriously as we potentially should. We peer into other's critiques of the person with a blind eye to logic. If someone close to us is critical of an aspect of our dating partner, we reject him or her because of the tunnel vision of emotion and love versus the steady hand that is tempered in rationalizing whom we are dating.

If you listen, truly listen, to others around you without judgment or condemning what they are telling you (some will be critical) you may gain some insight into what you do not see. Therefore, before you are quick to reject the consumer reviews of your potential spouse "read" and take the time to ponder them. You do not have to admit the other is right or wrong, but you do have to look at the caution signs on the road ahead if they tell you what is in front of you.

What Kind of Cars Have You Purchased in the Past?

If I were to tell you that I purchased the same brand and style of car each time for the last several years despite the fact that they always broke down, had frequent recalls, and had an abysmal safety record, what would you tell me?

You would say that I was likely not the smartest consumer for picking the same poor quality car company over again and again, right? I might reply to you something like, "Well, I am comfortable with the car, I know all of its faults, sounds, and where all the gauges, knobs and buttons are."

Still, comfort in a relationship does not necessarily mean a satisfying partnership. I may be comfortable in the worn in seat of my car, but does that mean it good for my back? Does that reveal it is the best thing for me? Does it suggest I could not find anything better?

In addition, if I am seeking out the same type of vehicle/person to date why is that? Why am I in search of the same attributes that are not working out for me? Why do I find a potential partner with a different face but the same qualities and issues? Likely, you would also begin to have less sympathy for me for not recognizing that banging my head against the same wall leads to the same consequence each and every time.

Reputation is Important:

When you look for a vehicle you may also look at the reputation of the company; what is the safety record, reliability, history?

When you are in the early stages of a relationship you may not see the importance of history, however, the past will tell you far more than the words spoken to you. Look for the actions and choices the person made in the past. In short, look for the history and reputation that the person has autographed their past with, as this will be most indicative of what you can predict in the writing of your relational future.

Who Stands Behind the Car?

When I purchase a car I look for not just the car, but do I like the dealership? Are they trustworthy? What is the climate of the place? Do I like the mechanics, sales people, secretaries, and the service counselors? In short, are they going to stand behind my investment or not?

Similarly, when you engage in a relationship you are not just joining a partnership with a spouse/boyfriend/girlfriend. You are joining an extended family who will be more or less involved in your life should a future evolve.

Do you "click" with them and do they join with you? If they do not, it may be easy initially to dismiss this as unimportant. However, remember that the more involved you become the more that you may be drawn into the larger extended family. There is a reason why jokes about in-laws have been the punch line of many a comedian.

The Three Relational Triple A's Are Not for Towing or Pulling You Out of a Difficult Spot. They Are the Hazard Lights of a Relationship:

We have often heard of the three A's as a "club" that assists in rescuing us from a flat tire, a dead battery, or (in the past) giving us directions of how to get to a location when we needed help in planning trip.

The "Relational Triple A's" are those of **A**busive Behaviors, **A**ffairs outside the relationship and **A**ddictive Behaviors in usage of illicit substances. These are of such danger that they steer a relationship right into a virtual brick wall at 100 mph, and simply cannot lead to the growth of a healthy relationship, or can lead to very real physical or emotional harm.

You may say, well, we are an exception. Nope, it is just a matter of time before the train catches up with you and destroy one or both of you if you don't directly (and strongly) address these issues aggressively.

Don't Buy a Self-Driving Car:

This is a technology that is still not yet perfected, but you can buy a self-driving car if you have the money and take that risk. I was discussing with someone who has been in one about what the experience is like. He said, "Well the car does drive itself. However, you have to always be paying attention in case the car makes a mistake or an error. That way you can get your hands on the wheel and correct any problem before it is too late."

Relationships are kind of like the issues many have with the self-driving car. They do not steer themselves and require attention, time, and energy. If you do not have the time or energy to invest fully in the relationship, or you still need the time to invest in yourself, don't begin one. Do not take time to make this vital investment until you are fully ready to grab the steering wheel and put the complete attention and energy necessary for success.

How Does the Car Handle in Snow, Rain or Other Emergent Situations?

Despite what the manufacturer tells you about how a car handles in hazardous weather, the true test is when you are driving across a snow swept road. It is when you have tightly white knuckled the steering wheel that you truly determine your vehicle's ability to handle the perilous path ahead of you.

Similarly, testing how a prospective mate reacts in a stressful situation tells a lot. Does the person, yell, scream, shut down, or place blame on someone else (like you)? This is a good litmus test of how they may react in stressful situations.

The Vehicle Warranty:

When you purchase a vehicle, the dealer will offer you varying kinds of warranties to protect your investment. Some are of the platinum plan type while other are only bronze. What you may find in all of them is that they simply do not cover what goes wrong with your car.

With relationships, they have no guarantee that comes with them. You, hopefully, become educated and before you give your heart fully, you stop and think about what you want in a relationship. There is both investment and significant emotional risk plan consequently.

Lesson 1: Don't Settle… This Is A Big Purchase-
Get What You Want or Save Up for It

The best possible way to inoculate yourself against continued failed relationships is to know what you want, know what you don't want, and know the signs of when you are on the right road and when you are about to crash.

Overview:

The journey ahead is a long one, but worthwhile, if ultimately you find the soul mate for which to ride shoulder to shoulder with in this road trip called life. I ask that you keep your mind open and think about those that you have met to see how they fall into the chapters ahead.

More importantly, I ask you to be honest with yourself as we discuss the types of prospective partners that we will address. After all, this book is about you and despite, what others will tell you about your life, ultimately driving your own life.

Lesson 2:
Look for a Long Term Partner Not a Sports Car.

"Relationships, like cars, should undergo regular services to make sure they are still roadworthy."

--Zygmunt Bauman

Have you ever heard that you find love when you are least expecting it? Well in many cases that may be true. Now, perhaps, you may have not wanted to hear this. You are reading a book on finding a relationship and are actively seeking a partner.

Well, the point of why I tell you this is the reason has some validity. Many of us have preconceived concepts of what we are looking for in a spouse or partner. Initially, the only gauge we have of this is by the looking on the external appearance of who someone is. This is why on-line dating is so appealing. You can gaze at the outside of someone at first impression with some vaguely accurate characteristics and traits. From this superficial data, you can make a less than informed decision.

The result? Many times by just solely looking on the exterior aspects of a relationship, it is doomed to fail. Another case and point? Look at the rash of reality shows over the last several years. Good-looking people, going to beautiful looking tropical destinations, only to succumb to ugly looking breakups splashed on the tabloids a few months later.

Are we surprised by this result? They do not likely even know each other's favorite color and they are "buying the car" based on how sporty, sexy, and sleek the outer body looks. Are they ready for the days when the other is sick and looks like a sports car that has gone off-roading in the mud storm of the flu or life? Likely not.

The Body of the Car Changes:

This one is a simple unpleasant fact. One day you (and your prospective partner) will wake up and you will be old. You will likely be a little broader around the middle or the bottom, have more hair in places you don't want it, and less hair in places you do. Smooth skin will become wrinkled, and no matter how much you exercise and watch your diet you will eventually slow down.

When you meet a prospective partner count how many times you say, "they are beautiful, hot, gorgeous... (Whatever your chosen description of physical attractiveness you choose to add)." Now, close your eyes and ask yourself again, if I could not see them would I find as attractive the body of that person's soul, as that of their physique?

The Muscle Car, Biker, and "the Bad Boy":

In my counseling in numerous settings, I have found a fair number of people (usually women) who are attracted to the motorcycle, tough riding, bad boy. These guys are tough, gruff, and some have their fair share of baggage that they place in the pockets of their bikes or muscle cars.

The goal in these relationships goes something like this: "He is a challenge. I like the brave and audacious nature he harbors; I can 'tame' him. If I do what no one else could do (or had done) what a major accomplishment that will be!" It is like the horse trainer who attempts to domesticate a wild stallion…can I meet the challenge or fail trying?

The logic may make some sense in the short-term. The issue is that relationships are a great deal of work in the best of circumstances. If one partner is working harder than the other is at the partnership in the short-term it may survive. However, if you are constantly the one steering the relationship and putting the time and effort in it will eventually dissolve. Alternatively, just as bad, you will become resentful at some point in the future when you recognize you are putting all the fuel in the relationship and the other is mostly taking and not putting gas back into the virtual tank.

Haven't You Learned Anything About Buying the Right Car All These Years Later?

When you purchased your first car, you probably did not have much experience in the process of buying a car. You may have been one who was easily swindled, not known the financing options that were available, or were impulsively ready to buy any car on the lot that even remotely met your needs.

Now, after a few cars you are experienced and demonstrate more wisdom; you are more restrained (not purchasing the very first car you see), you are able to "talk the talk" of buying a vehicle and are more skeptical if a slick salesmen tries to dupe you into the first set of wheels you set your eyes upon. In short, you are applying a different strategy to the same situation because you have learned the hard way to think and act better.

In relationships, some of us use the same strategy for meeting mates that we have used when we were in our late teens/early twenties. The difficulty is, as you mature, so should your relational strategies.

This means that:

- Looking less at the physical and more towards the emotional.
- Expanding outside the nightclub and bar scene to places that are more likely to have others that demonstrate common values of what one is looking for.
- Striving more for shared values and less for looks.
- Eliminating those that are just "players" (i.e. those that are seeking superficial or solely physically based relationships).
- Making relational decisions based on a future with someone than for what is okay for today.
- Seeking a partner who has a history of success in life versus success in smooth talking.

When You Buy a Sports Car You Are Buying an Image:

Before we purchase a car (or almost anything), we are often enticed by an image. The commercials of the wind blowing in your hair, driving down the Pacific Coast Highway, sun beaming. It is an image, a dream, a fantasy; and so it is with an image that some people purchase, thinking that this aura will somehow project down upon them in as if by magic.

One assumes because the person looks good on the outside or is a smooth talker they can buy the "image" and what is promised. It may look good as an escape from your stresses of life, bills, and the ugliness of what you are experiencing that keeps you from the ideal life you would like.

What you are looking for is not a "dream," or a commercial of a utopian life. You are seeking traits, values, and an ability to relate below this superficial surface. If you buy only into the outward appearance you will begin a relationship teetering on the edge as it will only be superficial in nature.

A Sports Car is Not Always the Most Reliable:

My father, after many months of research, purchased a reliable car. It was not pretty in the least, the color was okay, but it was certainly nothing to look at. Yet, in the coldest of days, the car started, in the worst of weather the car got us there. For fifteen years the car took us where we needed to be, faithfully.

Flash forward twenty-five years, and my son on an impulsive buy, purchased a sporty looking vehicle. I loved the way it looked (as did he of course). He would gaze outside the house and look at it in the driveway with his eyes glazed over with pride. It was his arm candy, his pride and joy, his "trophy" of sorts.

The only problem is under the hood, it rattled, shook, and when you turned the key, you had the 50/50 chance that it may, or may not, start. When he had to go to work, he worried whether it would be able to get him there or if he would have to ask a friend for a ride or us. He would then be forced to tell his job of his car troubles and hope it did not look like some lame excuse for his being late.

Sound like a few relationships you know? Some of us have to make excuses for our partner because they are not reliable. If you have to make excuses because someone is not reliable and then rationalize, or minimize, why this is the case then you are committing a cardinal rule of poor relational management…you are lying to yourself.

If you are making up justifications for a partner to others or have to veil your relationship in a cloak of untruths this creates cracks in the starting relationship foundation. The excuses can gradually grow to half-truths, or to outright lies.

How do we know then that we have the reliable partner versus only the sports car model?

Look for the following:

1. Can you count on where they say they are going to be and when they say they are going to be there? I am not talking about procrastinating, that is different. What I am asking is when they are supposed to be somewhere are they at least making a justifiable attempt?
2. Do they have a job? Do they go to their job reliably?
3. Do they answer questions directly? Or, instead, do they dilute their statements with nondirective, misleading or intentionally vague statements?
4. When the going gets tough and arguing ensues, does your partner stay to resolve the conflict or return in a prompt fashion to attempt to get to the bottom of the issue? Conversely, do they leave, hold a grudge, react aggressively, or blame you?
5. Is the only reliability you see in physically/sexually context(s)?
6. Do they tell you "half-truths" or lie by omission (i.e. forgetting to tell you some major portion of their accounting of an important situation/issue)?

7. Believe actions, not words or statements. It is easy to say empty things, it is much more binding and difficult to "put your money were your mouth is."

Are You Guilty of "False" Advertising?

Another sign of this is what I call, "social media fairy tales." If you are posting pictures and statements based on what you "want" your relationship and life to look like to the world, and it is vastly off the path of what is actually going, on you may not be directly lying. Perhaps, however, it is worse for are you lying to yourself of what you are settling for?

If you are writing a fictional story of what you think your relationship is like and find yourself defending a fantasy romance novel recognize that the "dummy light" is flashing and blinking brightly. If, however, you find the story pairing up nicely with what is reality (this takes some time honestly thinking long and hard) you are on your way to building a strong foundation for a partnership.

Sports Cars Can Speed Through Relationships:

When a person is looking for a job and completing a résumé an integral part of the body of the document is the dates and timeframes of where you were at each respective job location. In fact, some résumé consultants suggest that if you have not been at a job for a notable period of time you shouldn't even put it on the résumé.

Why? Because the length of time you remain with an employer says something. It tells how loyal you are, how willing you are to stay steadfast when the going gets tough, and your ability ultimately to handle your chosen occupation and the stress that spills over in any vocational setting.

Sports car relationships do not have staying power. They start off fast, powerful, and passionate. On the flip side, is that they are short, quick, and can be relatively temporary and short-lived.

Therefore, developing a "mental résumé" of a potential partner is valuable. If you see a trail behind them of multiple short-term connections this should be an alert on your dating dashboard. Now, you can try to rationalize, "Well that was the past…I will be different." Just be aware that multiple short-term relationships have a common denominator and you are looking right into his eyes.

Sporty Cars Generally Have Sporty Egos:

To have a strong bond with a prospective partner they must be able to empathize. The antithesis of this skill occurs when an ego is so great it eclipses the ability to identify with the needs, desires, and wants of the person they are dating.

If you find yourself telling your boyfriend something important to you and each time he seems disinterested or not listening; hear the message he is subtly (or loudly) relaying to you. Count the amount of questions asked to you, notice the number of phrases that begin with, "I's and me's." Do not only look that a conversation is flowing; but is it flowing around, past, and over you and has very little to do with you? If it is, you have been run over with the sporty ego of the sports car partner. If the only question they ask you is, "How do you like my hair? Run!

Some Sports Cars Run Hotter:

If you have been driving down the road and see the hood of a vehicle open and steam billowing out of the car on the shoulder, you know the dangers of a car overheating. With a sports car built for speed, it also has to be prepared to handle the heat generated from such an aptitude.

In a relationship, heat has its place, we call it passion, and it can be the catalyst for sparking a fire in the joining of two people. The issue becomes that if the fire burns too hot the emotional reactivity of issues such as anger and temper ignite.

Anger is not necessarily a bad thing in a bonding between two partners. In fact, in my work, I have found that it is not the couple who show emotion in their interactions that are in the death throes of their connection. On the contrary, in these relationships there is still feelings and, hence, some degree of connectivity and caring bound up in that couple's emotions.

It is when couples come in devoid of any reaction or emotion that the relationship is most at peril. They have resigned themselves to not invest any more of their heart or feelings into the relationship and have put up a wall that is allowing them emotionally to move on. This tactic is, perhaps, a means of healing, but it designates that a vital element of the spark necessary to continue a connection (that of emotional investment) has extinguished.

Sometimes, emotional reactivity with sports car partners can run so hot, so quickly, that the passion fizzles out like a fire now snuffing out its very existence with no more fuel to burn. This is why we see romance based solely on passion quickly go the way of a badly written romance novel.

If the bond burns too hot constantly, it can begin to engulf the partnership that joins the couple who are together. The person who is continuously heated represents a very scary threat for the person on the other side of the flame. Just as in a real fire, it may start as a small plume of smoke that is hardly noticed. Then, a gray stream and, if not managed, eventually becomes an orange inferno that engulfs all around it.

Be aware of anger as it may start off with tacit signs that you "shoo away" in the tunnel vision of new love. Missing these, however, only leads to a larger warning sign down the road.

You Can Never Catch a Speeding Sports Car...But Do You Really Want to?

If you are looking to seek a long-term mate don't do it for the sport of it. Many times the person we are seeking tells more about us than it does them.

When you seek a person based on superficial values and for the challenge of it, what you find is that you are motivated to "win" their affection. It is akin to a person who sits with their eyes glazed over and play the slot machines for endless hours at a time.

They lose thousands, and the jingle of a hundred dollars' worth of coins make them think they are "lucky." How lucky is losing $2,900 dollars and getting $100 back? I would dare say, not very lucky at all.

The gambler may beg to differ because the inconsistent reinforcement of "winning" something means they are pursuing the challenge of getting back something, anything, in their investment. In psychology, they even have a term called the "Gambler's Fallacy" and denotes that "if something happens less frequently than normal during some period, it will happen more frequently in the future to balance out the odds."[2]

This is a very similar premise to that of what someone going for the sole challenge of a relationship with the superficially charismatic potential partner. You are going after the gamble that you will get something back in the connection (no matter how minute).

If you are the one always following and investing only to pull the proverbial handle and get a few coins in return-- you are losing. When you are investing 110%, to get 20% back in relational reward, this is a recipe for failure. Pursuing that relationship will leave you emotionally penniless and broke more quickly than not.

Just A Reminder…The Dings and Dents Show Up in the Sports Car Too:

I am a fan of pro football. Watching these athletes at the prime of their game is amazing. They are massive behemoths in top physical condition and strength, are far quicker, more powerful, and agile then the athletes only a decade or so in the past.

---

[2] "Gambler's fallacy." *Wikipedia*. Wikimedia Foundation, 07 Apr. 2017. Web. 26 Apr. 2017.

Look at the athletes of the past, however, and it tells a different story. They, in many cases, are older, heavier, sorer and slower than those peers who did not play football. The exterior that was once polished, primed and new has given way to a beaten, dented and rusting surface that yields to body that is riddled with age and physical abuse at the hands of their career.

So, it is with the partner that you admire due to the outside beauty. They will eventually become fatter, balder, older, and less attractive. What you are left with is what you truly have for the long haul. Ask yourself are the values, personality, and compatibility able to carry us past the initial 3 year, 30,000 milepost that is marital/relational life?

If I were suddenly to be color blind to the outside color I love, would I still be able to fall in love with the whole picture?

Wanting A Sports Car Says More About You:

If you are looking for a partner solely for the surface appearance of your relationship that is saying more about you then them. This is not an easy reality to tolerate for some.

The key to a relationship, however, is honesty. Not only honesty in the dialogue and trust between the two involved in the partnership; but also honesty (and most importantly) truthfulness within yourself.

Ask yourself these difficult questions:

1- If this person was not good looking what qualities would I still be enthralled with?

2- If this person were to be unemployed tomorrow, would I find them less attractive?

3- Do I like them simply because they like me?

If you are answering "no" to these statements, you may be as to the preference towards more superficial relationship interactions.

Watch Out for Special Introductory Offers:

At times, when you are about to make a large investment like a car, you are given offers to sweeten the deal and draw you in even further. From gift cards, to free meals, to impossibly low finance offers these all help to push you over the edge when you are "on the fence" as to if you should invest your hard earned money into a particular car.

It is a similar parallel with the "sports car" relationship. You are given introductory offers to help pull you into the relationship. It can cause, "relational blindness," in which gifts or excessive empty flattering, create a tunnel vision in which you create, an unrealistic, yet magnetic world at which you believe you are the center.

How do you know if you are getting introductory offers?

1. Excessive expensive gifts without any notable reason.
2. Gifts that show expense without any attention to detail tailored specific to who you are or your idiosyncratic relationship.
3. Excessive gifts in the beginning of your time together that drift off (instead of vice versa).

4. Flattering comments that seem to be "over the top" without any direct connection to your personality, aptitudes, behaviors, or actions in the relationship.

Sports Cars Move Fast:

These people like to move fast and often have difficulty accepting rules or boundaries that you may try to set down. They tend to have difficulty recognizing details that indicate your interest (or lack thereof) because they are moving too quickly to notice subtle signs of what you need, want, or do not want to provide.

Ultimately, however, this is in an inability or lack of concern and empathy of what your needs are. It is a rush to get what the sports car partner wants and comes across as a lack of concern for your own needs and reassurances.

They are also hard to pin down. This person may ask you questions about you, but tell you perilously little about their friends, family or other connections. They keep you at "arm's length" in most aspects of their life and do not have any interest in giving you access to their internet and social media relationships or keep multiple social media accounts. They explain that their relationships outside of yours are kept with vigilant privacy. Concurrently, they are constantly on guard to anything that may expose their lifestyle outside of yours with them.

Have you ever run when you are with your pet dog? Notice they chase after you? That is the nature of these relationships. If you are always chasing, you are going to be doing a lot of running until you cannot keep up and bend over winded as well as exhausted. If you are always "chasing" the relationship, stop, and see if he/she turns around and returns to you. If he does not, do not catch your breath and run again after them. Run the other way to something better—be better, not eventually bitter.

The Sports Car Relationship Is Full of Good Marketing but the Gas Tank Is Empty on Action(s):

In any relationship, actions are much louder than words. This is nowhere more important than if you suspect a "sports car" relationship. If you are in a relationship with a "sports car", they are great at marketing themselves and telling you what you are seeking in a relationship. Look at actions and tangible proof and ignore mere words. One can tell you they are going to put gas in your car or change your oil but if they do not your car still stalls or your engine eventually blows up. It is your choice to simply hear what you want to hear or see what you need to see.

The Sports Car Companion May Always Have His/her Eyes On the Road:

When you are with a partner…it is your belief and hope that you are there with that partner. However, with a sports car partner their eyes are always looking down the road. Now, all of us have a tendency to look at attractive people. This being said, however, we have our focus on the person that is right beside us.

With a "Sports Car", they are always glancing and looking at what possibilities are around them. They have a deficit in attention of focus of the potential partner that sits right beside them. They have a chronic case of "the grass is always greener" and they cannot help but look at whose potential lawn they can wander onto next.

With this in mind, they are reluctant to verbalize out in public any indication that you are a couple. This will be paralleled in that they will not tell anyone that you are a couple in any manner or post any pictures or indication that you two have an intimate connection (despite assuring you otherwise).

Sports Cars Often Are Showy with Everything Except Your Relationship:

When you are in a new relationship, or in love, you want to be proud of your partner. You want to introduce them to everyone and yell out to the world, "Look who I am with!" Your relationship is a source of happiness and elation that others cannot help to see when they are around you both.

Interestingly, in the sports car relationship they are showy and boastful about almost everything. The "almost" is when it comes to your relationship itself; that is kept on "the down low," it is stunningly discreet. Why? Because they know if they address the relationship loudly, it officially makes a statement to others that they are off the proverbial market.

Remember, they are always looking around to scan potential connections with others. If they are discussing that, they are committed to another they believe the other lawns are now off limit to trespass upon.

Are You Proud to Show Off You Sports Car to Your Family?

Have you ever made an extravagant or foolish purchase only to hide it from your parents for fear of the well-deserved criticism? Parents have a way of bringing us back down to earth as quickly as a pin popping a helium balloon. They can make any of us, no matter our age, feel like five again.

With these particular types of connections, it is critical that you get outside, honest opinions. It is all too easy to rationalize what these types of persons tell you, minimize when you see aspects on the contrary, and vigorously convince yourself otherwise when your eyes tell you different.

It is hard to hear, but listen to what family, friends, and others say to you about these relationships. You do not have to admit they are right; just ponder what they are saying and be honest with yourself...completely honest.

Be Aware of Buyer's Remorse:

Remember when you were a kid and you wanted to get the latest and greatest toy? You dreamt about it, your parents lined up for it, and everyone spent more money than the retail price after waiting hours in lines going from store to store only to find it sold out at every possible location.

Then you got it, you were excited that you were the very first on your block to have it. Then as quickly as you were obsessed with it, you put it down only to let it collect dust with the other toys of your youth.

Sometimes we are caught up with the excitement of the challenge, only to realize once we get what we thought we wanted it fell short of our dreams and lofty expectations. This is a direct correlation to "sporty" relationships. You spend the time exerting all of your effort and attention towards a relational goal. When you secure the relationship you find the motivation and excitement diminish as you suddenly realize that the prospective spouse is not all you thought they were cracked up to be.

How to Handle a Sports Car:

If you are going to handle a sports car, it requires a certain amount of ability that varies from other cars in the lot. It is not for everybody and, in fact, the relationship can be fast and dangerous leaving you in the dust despite your best efforts to hold onto the relational steering wheel.

Here are some suggestions, however, if you choose to take the risk and spur on the excitement of the sports car that you have found in the car lot:

1- You pace the speed of the relationship: In these relationships, there will be a great deal of pressure for you to follow the frenetic tempo of these interactions. Do not be lured into this, you control the speed and keep your boundaries and expectations strong. If you take a step into this relationship, be cautious because you want your partner to know that you are giving a step does not mean you are allowing anything more than that.

2- Require honesty through actions not words: Look for actions that indicate what your partner is saying. When you see actions such as when you are made a priority over others and their plans only then you can justify relational progress.

3- Keep A Healthy Guard Up: Do not immediately lead in the dance with this relationship. See which steps they take first and remain cautious with your emotions. See how your relationship is classified when he/she explains the relationship to others. Is it vague and noncommittal? Is it proud and loud? If it is not the latter, it is time to put up a wall and question why this is?

4- Make your values clear early: When you do not immediately make known and clear your relational values (will discuss those more clearly later) you will be pushed away from them. If you continue down that road, you will eventually be painted into a corner in which you may have no choice but to forcibly state values that you previously did not make clear were important to you. This in turn, leads to confusion and frustration from the partner who did not know these were vital to you because you did not shed light on them sooner.

5- Avoid falling in love with labels: We sometimes become enamored with labels such as "attractive, successful, etc." If you fall in love with the label, it is akin to liking a brand name, simply for the sake of the name. A luxury car is nice to have but if does not drive, requires so much fuel you can't get anywhere, or is falling apart where is the luxury in that?

Lesson 3:
When You Are Looking for a Husband
Put On Your Headlights in The Tunnel,
Watch Your Dash
Beware of the Dummy Lights...

"It is a good thing to learn caution from the misfortunes of others."
--Publilius Syrus

When you are driving at night, you put on your headlights to see what is around you. Alternatively, you could drive and hope that the limited vision you have from the streetlights will suffice to getting you to your destination. Most of us don't do that though…why?

We want to see as much ahead of us as possible to assure maximum safety when we are out on the road so we know what is in front of us. Similarly, when we are driving and our "check engine" light comes on we are often quick to listen for any changes, read the manual and, when necessary, go to the mechanic.

Yet, when we are "driving" the direction of our relationships, we often do the equivalent of forgetting to turn on our headlights, ignore the lights on the panel, or drive head long into trouble. When you accelerate without thinking, you are driven into a world of trouble in your car and in life.

Turning On Your Headlights:

When we turn on our headlights in our car, it vastly improves our peripheral vision. We can see the deer that are waiting nervously to cross in front of us on the side of the road, glimpse bicyclists, etc. In short, you are provided vital information that you would not otherwise view if you were simply looking at what you could glance directly in front of you.

In relationships, it is also helpful to see not just immediately in front of you. You may envision the perfect partner right next to you, due to your tunnel vision of the relationship. Yet, all the while, your friends and family are on the side of the road frantically waving to you to stay clear of the bridge-closed sign that you are barreling towards.

Listen to Your Friends and Family:

When you are in a relationship, you are emotionally invested; with the endorphins and strong emotional connections, that your brain generates there is a belief that you are likely to be biochemically invested as well. Therefore, you are probably not the best person to make a rational and unbiased view of the potential spouse that lies (or even "lies") before you.

This is why you need your family and friends to act as the "headlights" to better illuminate what your mind may be blind towards. Now, you may say your mother, father, or friends never like the partners you pick. This may be true, but if the majority of those that you trust, respect, and know you best are telling you that this person is not the one for you…guess what? They are probably not the one for you.

Do not respond when those around you offer what you perceive as criticism…just listen and ponder. If you do react, you may be burning important bridges that you will need later for your support should the relationship go awry or the support that you would like for relationship if this person were to become a long-term partner.

Be aware, also that the more those that you love are telling you the potential partner is not the right one for you the more you may actually be drawn to that person. It is not generally rational; rather, it is a reactive emotional response. Nevertheless, at the end of the day, the strategy of "us against the world" may just leave you two against the world. Personally, I take the odds of the world winning out, to just two surviving

Use Your Headlights to See the Other Pedestrians on the Road:

When someone is trying to impress you, they can do a great job of masking things that they do not want you to see. All of us…and I mean all of us… hide certain aspects to put our best foot forward when we are first engaging in a relationship. Personally, I remember not taking my, then fiancée, for BBQ in fear that I would look like the utter slob I could be when eating a mouthful of ribs. Hence, I chose to not want her to see that part of me.

Like that example, most of what we choose to not highlight about ourselves to a potential mate is innocuous and in the long run not very significant. However, those that have bigger flaws or attributes that you may not be able to live with or tolerate also are also likely kept in the shadows. Hence, it is vital to see through other people's lenses a better and clearer perspective of the individual's character and fabric.

How Do They Treat Those That Can't Do Anything for Them?

Look at a person's relationships as a whole, not just the limited segment that they want you to see. Remember the scene in the Wizard of Oz when the wizard tells Dorothy and the others, "Don't look behind that curtain!" They look, and they see the true person, not the persona.

Looking behind the "curtain" of a person can tell you quite a lot. For instance, watch how the person treats the person pumping gas, the cashier, the waitress. Are they polite? Do they lose their patience easily? Are they demanding? When a mistake is made, do they tend to overly blame the person haplessly in front of them?

If you look at your prospective life partner during these times, you get an unvarnished view of the true person. Some of us are less likely to put up the veil of impressing their potential partner in these situations, however, can give you a more accurate telling of what the person is like.

Use Caution…However:

There is the old saying by Publilus Syrus, that "familiarity breeds contempt." In other words, the exact opposite of the above can be true too. That is, people tend to be nicer to strangers than they are to those closest to them.

It is a strange, but true, paradox of human nature. Think about it, you say negative things to your significant other, children, family, and even close friends that you would not say to others both good and bad. You would likely never insult the person delivering your pizza and yet, you may say some of the meanest and most hurtful things to those that are supposedly closest to you.

This means that when you are evaluating the person you are in a relationship you must not only check around the exterior relationships, but also the interior and closer bonds that the person keeps. These are generally, of course, more telling than the superficial relationship addressed above.

Do They Have Friends? How Long Have They Been Friends? What Do They Share in Common?

First off, if your prospective mate does not have friends question the reason why? Is it they cannot maintain a bond with another? Do they have significant social issues? This is important, because it tells you how they handle relationships in general. Additionally, if you have a circle of friends, and they don't, will jealousy rear its ugly head when it comes time to you balancing your time with your friends?

If they have a history of short-term friendships (less than seven years) and they are constantly making new friends while discarding the old, that can be an omen for how the handle relationships in general. It is not a sole "dummy light" but it should be kept in the back of your pocket to analyze later.

That Annoying Seat Belt Light Won't Shut Off:

Those that are impulsive may be fun during the outset of a relationship, as they are unpredictable, which adds a certain flavor and excitement to a burgeoning new relationship. It is nice to not know what you may be doing next at the outset.

That being said, impulsivity is something to be cautious about on the "dummy light" of relationships. If your potential partner acts without thinking as evidenced a history of spending without thinking, job moving due to excessive boredom or moving from relationship or place to place, this should set your "dummy light" blinking and sounding.

The Air Bag Light Is On:

This is a similar person to the "Seatbelt Light" mentioned above, except this is the person that is always looking for the next adrenaline rush and adventure. They are not looking in the moment; rather they are considering at the next adventure to hopscotch to and become bored easily when they do not have some thrilling task ahead.

The difficulty becomes then that this person will become easily bored in a relationship (any relationship) that does not constantly infuse an adrenaline rush. Unless, you are on a constant reality show the "air bag" relationship will soon deflate and move on to the next brief, fleeting, and exciting bond.

The Transmission Light Is Blaring:

Transmissions allow you to shift from one gear to another in a car. There is nothing worse than hearing the grinding of a slipping transmission that is unable to effortlessly change from one gear to another.

So, it is with relationships, look carefully to see how your prospective spouse handles situations that arise "out of the blue." Is he/she able to handle them in a proactive, productive, fashion? Alternatively, does he/she fall apart, become angry, blame you, or others, or handle it in some other negative and fruitless manner?

You may be quick to say, well how does this matter in the longer scheme of a relationship? Well, in any connection it will be tattered by the constant unpredictable nature of the world that surrounds it. How does a partner handle it? Are they going to self-destruct, attack the relationship, or join together to get through life's ups and downs? Knowing this question goes a long way to answering the vitality and longevity of a prospective partnership.

Watch for Low Windshield Fluid Warnings:

If your car runs out of windshield wiper fluid, it can get mighty hard to drive. As you cruise along the dirt, squashed bugs and any other item thrown at you at 50 plus miles per hour your vision becomes increasingly blurred.

It is the same in romance. If you continue to drive along seeking partnerships without clearing your vision first, you put yourself in danger of missing critical qualities of the relationships around you. It is vital to be able to stop and see the imagined forest for the trees.

Clean Your Windshield… So You Don't Miss:

- Is he/she always honest with you?
- Are you in love with the relationship or the person?
- Is he/she not just saying they care about you…but also showing it?
- Are you able to clearly look at the relationship from a logical as well as an emotional perspective?

Don't Compare Your Vehicle to That of Others:

Let's go back to the car lot of relationships. I want you to picture that you are given an unlimited supply of money. Credit, cash, the sky is the limit. Think, of the car you would get if money were not an object?

You would likely buy a luxury or sports car with every available feature and option available. No feature or option would be spared: anything that could be leather would be, anything that could be heated should be, any feature that might be on your dashboard has to be. Even your plates are personalized to "DREAMCAR1" to proudly indicate the investment in your material dreams that are reflected on the very chrome of your new dream mobile.

You are thoroughly satisfied and pleased with your new purchase and spend the next year looking at every gadget and feature of your new car. In fact, secretly, you gaze at your vehicle every few hours in your garage, to be sure, it is still there and to reassure yourself that this automotive work of art is actually yours.

Now, on your daily drive to show your "eye candy" to the hordes of admiring drivers on the road you come across a terrible sight; in the two years since you purchased your car they have come out with a new model, nicer colors, better features, and an even nicer body style to boot. In front of you is that new 2019 model; no longer is anyone looking at your car (not even you). You now have a case of deflating buyer's remorse as you do a visual comparison of what you wish your vehicle had in comparison to the one you stare at in front of you.

Comparison in the material world is always a dangerous proposition. In the continuum of the sphere of material wealth, you will always find someone who has more items or financial wealth than you. Therefore, comparison is an unhappy world of "looking over your shoulder" as to who is behind you while, simultaneously, climbing the next wrung of the ladder as to who you are trying to get above.

You may say how does this have to do anything with relationships? Well, if you are seeking to compare yourself or your relationship to those of others you are in for a similarly dangerous and slippery slope. Yet many of us find ourselves constantly vigilant; looking all around us in our society as to how our rapport and bond compares to that of others.

Here are the dangers and fallacies that are associated with relationship comparisons:

- Media gives a fantasy image of real relationships: Much of what we perceive in our dialog with others is what we see on television and on the internet. Even these so-called "reality" television shows are heavily peppered with editing and embellishment so that every relational interaction is filled with passion, vacations around the world, and dates that are more intricate then anything that most of us have been exposed to in our intimate relationships.

Even though you may know this is not realistic or practical this can provide you an unfair bar for which your relationships should meet.

- Social Media Is An Inaccurate Prism for Which Others Wish You to View and Judge:

    Most of us now engage those in our social circle primarily via social media. The difficulty is that these are fictional fables of what your "friends" on social media want you to see or where they might want their own relationships to look like.

Friends on social media are not likely to air out their own dirty laundry (unless the relationship has degraded to a point of significant conflict). This means that you will see the sanitized and "happily ever after" version of relationships. Everyone is happy, doing great things, with pictures of elaborate meals and messages publicly of both partners professing their undying romantic love for each other.

What you do not see is the stark underbelly in many partnerships. As a casual viewer, you do not see the daily minor (or major) conflicts, the crushing bills that comes with those extraordinary trips documented on social media, or the nights that a frozen dinner substitutes for the gourmet meal that they have photographed for all to drool over on social media.

Lesson 3: When You Are Looking for a Boyfriend or Spouse Put On Your Headlights in The Tunnel, Watch Your Dash

DO NOT compare your current or future relationships based on these unattainable standards that someone else has set. They are unrealistic and not sustainable if you use any of these as the yardstick for your relationship. Do not allow fictional fables of one's life to taint you're choosing or maintaining a relationship.

Lesson 4- You Are Not Just Buying the Person In Front of You ...Culture, In-Laws, and Religion

"A person without the knowledge of their past history, origin and culture is like a tree without roots. "

--Marcus Garvey

If you were in a boardroom of a marketing agency that was feverishly preparing a commercial for a major car manufacturer you would hear them discussing many details. Surprisingly, however, what you may find is that they may not talk about the actual car. Rather, they are talking about how to "sell" a philosophy, a lifestyle, a desire that purchasing from this company will provide. They want you to think it will lead to a life of you getting the perfect spouse, pulling up to a beautiful mansion, in which the perfect spouse meets you with the perfect two and a half children and the family dog. In short, they are selling you the well-known "American Dream."

And So... It Is With Relationships:

When you are seeking the right partner, you are not just buying "the car" so to speak, you are buying other bits and pieces as well. You are (maybe unwittingly) buying a culture, a religion, in-laws, bills, baggage, and much more. If you think that the person you are intending to connect with does not have any of these items or you can somehow separate them from this fabric of their being you may have more luck getting out ink stains from the upholstery of your own car seats.

Additionally, don't think that you do not bring to the table the same issues into the relationship. You can ignore these items for a period of time, however, they will be the background music that is constantly playing in the framework of your connection. It does not mean that if you have diverse viewpoints in any of these areas, most cannot be worked out. They very well may be; but they cannot be ignored or they grow and metastasis into deeper issues. Keep in mind, these concerns may not be able to be solved later when your bond has been established and grown upon a rocky and unsteady foundation if they are not thought about in the present.

Does Your Partner Stand Behind Their Warranty?

When you purchase a car they often have a plethora of warranties that they try to get you agree to pay a nominal fee for; there is the silver, gold, platinum, double platinum, and every other precious metal plan. One of the biggest complaints of these plans is that when a problem occurs you are told, "Sorry, your plan does not cover this…we do not stand behind that time of repair." The person then leaves frustrated and in a huff wondering why they wasted their time and money.

So, how does this correlate with your connection with a prospective partner? Well, when you have an issue with your boyfriend/girlfriend/fiancée/spouse do they support you? If you have a disagreement with their spouse (or your soon to be in-laws) do they stand up for you in front of the other person? Now, they may disagree with you later, but in front of that person they should be standing behind their investment… namely you! If they don't this can often lead to you being sold out whenever you need their support.

What If We Are Different Religions Can We Make It Work?

The Pew Research Center in 2015 found that "almost four-in-ten Americans (39%) who have married since 2010 have a spouse who is in a different religious group. By contrast, only 19% of those who wed before 1960 report being in a religious intermarriage.[3]" This is in contrast to, according to the Christian Science Monitor, in which mixed-faith partners "has shot up to 40 percent, from 20 percent in the 1960s."[4]

The question, I believe, is one of values. It is entirely possible to respect one's individual religion and work this out in the dynamic of a relationship; however, if you have divergent values with a potential spouse then your hope of having a mutually satisfying romance may indeed be miles apart.

For instance, can you answer the following questions regarding your values in terms of the bond you are both hoping to grow and nourish?

---

[3] Murphy, Caryle. "Interfaith Marriage Is Common in U.S., Particularly among the Recently Wed." *Pew Research Center*. Pew Research Center, 02 June 2015. Web. 13 Sep. 2016.
[4] Hanes, Stephanie. "Interfaith America: 'Being Both' Is a Rising Trend in the US." *The Christian Science Monitor*. The Christian Science Monitor, 23 Nov. 2014. Web. 26 Feb. 2017.

- What is your definition of family? How much alone time versus family time do you each need to feel fulfilled as a person, a couple and eventual family? How much time do each of you want/need with your friends?
- Do you have mutual friends? Do the majority of your friends like the respective partner?
- If you are going to have children what will be the dominant religion you will raise them? (Keeping in mind, it is extremely difficult to have a 50/50 religious split with your children).
- How important is work versus home life? What is the optimal balance for you both?
- Are you both able to insulate yourselves from the opinions and intervening of family and friends? Is it important to do this, or do you see your extended family as an offshoot of your relationship that have strong influence over you both?

The Culture of the Dealership:

Each job site has its own culture. It is what you feel when you come into the dealership of car sales as well as life. For instance, if the dealership's motto is "sell at any cost," then you will find a car dealer that may substitute honesty for sales numbers. If you are in a culture of trust and return business, a dealer may actually tell you that a particular car is not for you (even if it means potentially losing a sale).

We all are built on a woven fabric of culture as well. This is so ingrained in many of our natures that we may forget how deeply it runs though are choices and beliefs and may be of surprise when it butts up against a view that seems "commonsense" to us but fundamentally does not parallel with another person's culture or beliefs.

Know Your Relational Culture:

- Does your family or beliefs hold to more values that are traditional in which one person is "in charge" and the other one plays a subordinate role?
- Do you and your partner seek to understand divergent views on your culture or do you criticize or refuse to change/listen to the other, or become overly defensive?
- Assuming makes an "a** out of you and me": The thing about assumptions is that you take for granted things that maybe should not be taken for granted. Explain why you do what you do and why you do it. Do not assume that someone should "just know" how you feel or why you feel that way. No one, no matter how long you have been together, is a mind reader.
- Do you both want children? How important are children and a family to you both? If you do not agree on this critical crossroads; one, or both of you, will end up resentful of each other.
- How much alone, friend, family, and relational time does each of you feel you need and/or should have? Each of us has varying levels of time with each other, family, friends and alone time we need to feel fulfilled. If you do not agree on this one or both of you will feel that you are sacrificing important aspects of your lives.
- Are your priorities the same? In other areas of your life, such as career do you want the same aspirations? Does one of you want to be a stay-at-home parent or are you both looking to be hard charging career types? You can have anything you want...you

just cannot have everything you want at the same time, together, to the same degree always.

- Do you like each other's friends? Friendships are an important part of a couple's respective lives. It allows each partner an opportunity to develop supports outside of the relationship. If you do not like each other's friends, you will grow to resent each other and spending time with your corresponding friendships.

In-Laws: The Background Music That Plays: You DO Marry the Family…In Most Cases:

In most cases, your relationship does not exist in a vacuum. What I mean is that though the primary aspects of your relationship is between the two of you, it is not that simple. To one extent or another, you will be in contact with your partner's family.

How Well Is My Boyfriend Connected? Does My Prospective Partner Have Any Other Connections?

There is an old saying that you do not just marry your spouse…you also marry his/her in-laws as well as the extended family members. This is, dependent on the relationship(s), very true. Some partners are more involved and invested in their relationship then others. For instance, you (I hope) are very involved and have loving committed relationship with your parents and extended family.

Having such interactions are vital and should not be sacrificed at the hands of someone who seeks a bond with just you. None of us can garner everything we desire from one relationship. If so, we would never need friendships (or family connections for that matter).

Instead, we would put all of our eggs in the one and only basket of a single relationship. Unfortunately, this will not provide you everything you need in the long run however. No one single person has the ability to meet every solitary need you may have. No, you require family and external friendships for that necessity. On the flip side, your partner should have connections outside of their immediate relationship with you. If not, one must question, "Why does my partner not have any long term commitments in the form of family or friend connections with others?" That question should be deserving of a closer and skeptical look.

But...His Family Does Not Live Close By And/or He Does Not Speak With His Family:

So, you may think that if your significant other does not speak to his parents, that you are "off the hook," right? You will, of course, not have to relate with those external influences and are in the clear, right? Not necessarily.

Ask yourself the following questions if your significant other does not speak to his parents.

- Why doesn't he speak to his parents? Not speaking to someone close to you because of anger is a coping strategy (albeit a bad one). If this is the way he handles issues of conflict emotionally with those close to him, it may be foreshadowing in your own relationship of his coping skills.
- What does he do with all of that emotional baggage? Relationships are filled with a full array of emotions. They are like playing a game of "Whack-a-Mole" when you try to knock down the emotions in one area they often pop up somewhere else with a vengeance.

- If he has knocked down his anger, resentment, or other negative emotions somewhere else...will that mole "pop back up" in your relationship? It is something to think about, watch, and be on the lookout for.
- Does he defend his parents at all costs? It is important that in a relationship you are able to also preserve your vital family and friendship bonds. However, it is also a matter of priorities. If your boyfriend/significant other is always defending his parents at the peril of your own relationship, it is a sign that your relationship may not be number one in the future. This becomes problematic, because in relationships it is all about priorities (or lack thereof).
- Looking at how he treats his parents and how they regard each other is a potential crystal ball into your own relational future: If you want to get a basic idea of how your prospective spouse will treat you in your future together you need to look at their parents.

Why? Think about how they learned to model solving relationship problems, raising children, handling conflicts? These are all learned in a large part by watching your relationship with your parents.

True, some of us say, "I will never be like my parents!" But as an educated consumer of selecting the right relationship, is that important information to be aware of as well? Also, watching how your boyfriend or significant other interacts with his mother can give good insight to how he respects those of the opposite sex.

The Culture of Culture:

Whether you realize it or not, you are a part of a culture. Likely, you are part of several cultures in the melting pot that is the United

States. Being a member of a culture means that you may have varying thoughts on the concept of relationships.

When you are in a culture you may make the assumption that "doesn't everyone think this way?" Often that is because we have a cultural supposition that this way of thinking is just "common sense" or "general knowledge." Don't assume that just because you, your friends, or your family think a certain way that this is true for the majority of others (or your boyfriend in particular).

Ask Questions:

Sometimes you may accidentally violate another culture's norm while just being well intentioned. For instance as a male, one may think giving a handshake to a female of another culture is a sure sign of respect and equality.

In reality, in certain Islamic and Orthodox Jewish cultures it is forbidden for anyone to have physical contact with someone of the opposite gender that they are not related to. So, without even trying it easy to cross a cultural expectation. This may be an extreme example, but it is important to learn about your boyfriend's or potential partner's culture. Doing so, allows you to understand expectations, rules, and boundaries that are a part of his family's (and to a varying extent) his cultural beliefs. Asking questions will only educate and cannot hurt.

Different Cultures Handle Conflict in Different Ways:

If you are from the Northeast, an Italian-American, or Nonorthodox Jewish "culture," stereotypically, you tend to be more "touchy feely" in your relationships with others. Hugging, kissing, and physical contact among people is more accepted. Additionally, emotional expression is generally acknowledged among communications with others and questions that are more of a personal nature are generally permissible. If one is from another culture, physical contact with strangers may be less customary and more cautious, overt conflict or emotionally charged conversation is considered impolite or downright rude. Discussion is kept, initially, more superficial and cautious.

Which is correct? The answer is neither. However, if you come from a contrasting culture, you may be quick to label the other's views as "wrong" or uncomfortable. In psychology they often call this the fundamental attribution error which is our tendency to explain someone's behavior based on internal factors, such as personality or disposition, and to underestimate the influence that external factors (such as situational influences) have on another person's behavior. That is, we tend to not look at culture and instead take things personally and not examine the role of how someone's growing up might influence the way they handle things.

Let's take another car example, did you ever notice that those who are driving faster then you are "crazy" and those who are driving slower are "just idiots?" If you labeled people because they are driving faster or slower then you, what makes your speed the exact right way to travel? This is because you tend to "attribute" what others are doing to you directly and personally and that they are simply "wrong."

What Is Your Financial Culture?

In my time as a marriage and family therapist do you know what couples argue most about is? Money.

Why do couples argue about money? Because it is something that everyone has to work out...in our culture money is control and power. In relationships, control and power are likewise an issue that needs to be communicated and sorted out as to the level each partner has.

Who is going to do what? Who is going to spend the money on what? These are all important issues that need start to be ironed out BEFORE a relationship gets serious.

Now, each of us has a financial culture that we originate from. If you were lucky enough to come from a wealthy family, perhaps you do not consider money as an important factor because it simply has always been there. If you come from a family who struggled financially, then you may find that you are more frugal and cautious with how you spend what you have.

Ask yourself and your partner these questions to see if you are in a similar financial culture and begin to have the discussion of how to create your own unique financial lifestyle:

- When you were a child how did your parents spend money? Were they spenders or savers? How did the encourage you to save or spend money?
- How do you feel about credit cards? What is your belief about maintaining a balance on credit cards for something "we really want?"
- Do you think we should have checking and saving accounts that are joint or separate? Why?
- How much do you believe is important to save? Invest? Spend?
- Do you ever get worried or stressed about finances? How do you handle that?

- Have you ever made mistakes about money you regretted? If so, how did you handle them?
- How much money should be kept in case of an emergency?
- Who would you like to be in charge of the day to day paying of the bills? Which of us is better at this?
- Before we get married should we seek a financial/investment counselor for help?

These questions may seem uncomfortable, and they are certainly not always a pleasant or romantic discussion. What they are, however, are realistic ways of handling issues proactively. These questions are some of "the work" side of relationships which are extremely important in the long run.

In The World of Cultures What You Know Is Often Wrong:

- Simple activities like shaking of your head means "no" in most cultures. Except in India, where it actually means "yes."
- We laugh when we are happy in the U.S., in Japan it is often a sign that someone displays when they are embarrassed.
- In Europe, it is considered polite to be a half hour late for an event; in Germany it is thought of as rude not be punctual.
- In many Latin and Eastern cultures, it is known as impolite to "toot your own horn," not be a team player, and/or brag about your accomplishments or be forward in getting what you want. In the United States, this is generally not the case; independence and being a "go getter" is more important and considered a positive attribute.

Who Cares About This? Why Do I Need to Know About My Boyfriend's Culture?

How did you become who you are? How did you choose who you want to be with?

Each of us grew up in your own unique world. A world that is only, and exclusively, understood by you and the family that you were raised with. The idiosyncratic experiences in your being reared is what makes you who you each are. That, in a nutshell, is your culture.

If you want your significant other to understand you and put themselves "in your shoes." They must comprehend that distinctive culture from which you grew and came from. If you want to know that amazing person you are with the same should holds just as true.

If You Want Success…Do the Hard Work First:

Relationships, initially, are full of romance, passion, and excitement. It is important to treasure these times together as you are doing the vital work of building a strong romance between you both. That being said, if you want that foundation to last for many years ahead you must do the hard work to make sure that the foundation is strong first. That building is of sweat, work, and tears but in the end, it builds a monument you both can be very proud of.

Lesson 5- Opposites Attract in Car Batteries... Values Attract in Relationship

*"It's not hard to make decisions
when you know what your values are."*

--Roy E. Disney

Do Opposites Attract? Sure They Do, in Batteries:

Batteries are a good example of opposites attracting. How many times have we had a dead car battery "jumped" only to see the vehicle, as if by magic come to life? Connect the same polarity and what happens? Nothing, no spark...no life. So, is this the same with partnerships?

We have all heard that opposites attract. Most of us know couples who seem like polar opposites; one is outgoing the other shy and reserved, one is hard charging and reckless, the other cautious and empathetic. So do opposites REALLY attract each other in relationships?

That is an important lesson to know, now a more interesting question comes to light; do you look for partners that share common interests or avoid them and seek a partner in places and with attributes that are the polar opposite from your own? On the surface it may seem that we would seek those that have the opposite characteristics as us because, in doing so, we find become a more balanced whole with another person who has strengths to our weaknesses.

What the Studies Say:

A few years ago, two researchers, Nathan Hudson and Chris Fraley, sought to find the answer to this very question[5]. The investigators conducted a battery of comprehensive tests. Every other month on a diverse sample of 174 couples from all different cultures, races, and sexual orientations they tested relationship quality. In the exams, they looked at a number of personality markers to determine the couples' satisfaction within their respective relationships.

In doing so, they looked at a hallmark of key factors such as *how outgoing each partner was, how amenable they were to each other, perfectionism, their level of emotional stability* and *desire to seek and try new experiences.* In addition, the couples each completed a screening several times during the study to determine their degree of satisfaction in their respective relationships.

What the research found was that the answer was not a simple one. Couples demonstrated similar levels of kindness and were similar in emotional stability were, generally, more satisfied in their relationships. By contrast, sharing the others traits studied had no effect on their perceived relationship quality.

---

[5] Hudson, Nathan W., and R. Chris Fraley. "Partner similarity matters for the insecure: Attachment orientations moderate the association between similarity in partners' personality traits and relationship satisfaction." *Journal of Research in Personality* 53 (2014): 112-23. Web.

Values Are a Constant:

One of the areas that should be a constant, is that of your values. As a couple, you may have vastly different personalities, however, if your general mission is the same or similar it can lead to a very satisfying long-term relationship.

Think about work. In any given organization, you have many people with diverse personality types, beliefs, and cultures. Yet, somehow, all of these parties are able to work within their various perspectives in how they view things and not only survive, but thrive! Why? Because they can set aside traits for values. They put on the back burner, for the most part, the trivial differences for the values of doing something for a bigger purpose for the company's mission.

What Are Your Values, What Are Your Priorities?

Let us pretend that you are given 100,000 dollars and asked to invest it among several different accounts. How would you decide? Where would you deposit your money? Would you invest it all in one area and be risky, or take the funds and spread them around for stability, but less of a gain?

However, and whatever, you decide would be based on your priorities. There is no right or wrong answer, rather, it is just what you choose of how you are going to answer those many areas in life that are not simply "black and white" but are in "many shades of gray."

So What Are Your Priorities?

Imagine a day where you are at 100%; you are not burdened by anything at all. You feel your best, you can focus your best, and you are at your best in all of your relationships. Of course, some days (or many days), we may not be at 100%, but on this day you are at your prime.

Now that 100% must be split…you have to devote that time among all the facets in your life that you find important.

What A Typical List of Priorities May Include (in Order):
1. Individual Health (Emotional and Physical)
2. Your relationship with your significant other
3. Family (Immediate)
4. Extended Family
5. Career
6. Friends
7. Bills/Caring for the House
8. Community Obligations
9. Religious Obligations

So where do you split that 100%? You may say, "Well I will give 100% to my partner relationship." If you do, then can you afford the effects on your career or health? You may say, "I give 50% to my friends and 50% to my significant other." Well then, how do you deal with nagging guilt of a parent who says that you have not spent any time with them?

As you can see, splitting of your time is not easy. This means that you have to be certain that you do this in a manner that is best for your own emotional, social, and physical well-being. Sometimes, we feel bad because we are trying to go in a hundred different directions to make everyone else happy. The problem is you then only give a small percent to each of the areas that are important to you and, in turn, you make no one satisfied (most importantly yourself).

What Are Your Relationship Attribute Values Priorities? What Do These Words Mean To YOU?

1. Honesty: Can you tell each other anything? Are you truthful or do you tell "little white lies?"
2. Commitment: Do you put each other first? Will you still be attracted to something below skin deep when he/she is fat, bald, hairy, sick, or grumpy?
3. Forgiveness: When you irritate or hurt each other's feelings will you be able to get past that? Or, will you hold on to it to beat each other over the head with it later?
4. Fairness: Will you consider being fair to yourself and your partner (even if it is inconvenient at times)? Remember fair can never mean equal. In a relationship, each partner gives to the relationship what the other needs when they need it. Relationships then are like a balance scale or "see-saw" in which each partner may provide more at times. In the end, however, it relatively balances out.
5. Respect: Will you be able to show and display respect or will you resort to name calling, insulting, or demeaning your partner?
6. Trustworthiness: Can you count on each other to do what each of you say you will do and/or be there for each other?

The above questions are some of those that the relationship must hold as important if the couple is to survive over the long

haul. These are the traits that carry a relationship through the dings and dents of life as well as the bigger crashes.

Values: Which of These Are Most Important?

We all have a value structure; however, if you are seeking a partner you are now trying to match up two individual value systems simultaneously. The circumstance then becomes, which are the values that you consider most vital in your shared lifestyles.

What are your top ten (in order), in terms of values? Look at Figure 1.0 below.

How do these complement those of your prospective spouse? Are they close, or nowhere on the same planet? (Please note, these are a sampling of hundreds of potential values).

Compassion	Friendships	Work	Humor
Achievement	Community	Friends	Wealth
Spirituality	Respect	Passion	Compassion
Security	Comfort	Outward Beauty	Success
Kindness	Contentment	Ambition	Dependability
Challenge	Decisiveness	Loyalty	Altruism
Calmness	Financial Independence	Fun	Education Level
Family**	**Parenting ****	**Finances****	**Faith****

** The bottom row are generally the most crucial of the value systems in a relationship.

How Does Your Priority System Match Up with Your Significant Other's?

Now once you have determined where you want to place your "eggs" in the baskets of priorities (hopefully you did not place all your priority eggs in one basket). Ask your significant other the same question. You can do this either formally or watch their actions, which as they say, "speaks far louder than words."
Which does he/she choose to place their 100%?

Look at what your partner finds important. Do they prefer you over their friends generally? Is their family for the, most part, more important than their career, or vice versa? Imagine how they complete this list of priorities and then answer the question if their priorities match up to your own. If they don't how are you going to reconcile this.
Remember, that people choose their priorities for the most part. If situations such as illness or job duties come up out of the blue then sometimes your priorities may shift for a temporary period of time. But then the question becomes, over the long haul do those priorities match up with yours?

Begin with an Eye Towards the Ending Goal:

For years, you have been planning and hoping for your ideal relationship. What are you looking for? What do you aspire it will be like?

I don't mean what the wedding will be like. Many times, we become obsessed with the day. What kind of flowers? What kind of food? Who is going to be invited? Where will the wedding be? Will we have a destination wedding?

With all of these thoughts on one day, we develop tunnel vision as to the many days of happiness that are supposed to proceed that single event. In the end, those following days and years are infinitely more important. Now, you may say, "This is my special day! It is going to be the best day ever…it is about me!" That is true, but if it is not about the couple then your prospective spouse is about as replaceable as the bride and groom cake topper that adorns the wedding cake…isn't he/she?

Instead, look at how you are going to make a marital life versus a wedding day. You are at point A (now) and you know point B (the end). The vital element is how do you connect the two? That very connecting line of life becomes the lofty mission ahead.

To Develop Your Relationship Mission Statement:

If you go to just about any company or business, you will find that they have a mission statement emblazoned somewhere. The mission statement is a simple mantra that encapsulates what the organization "is about;" it is a detailing of thoughts, hopes, and ambitions in a "nut shell" format.

Ask yourself the following and develop them in a Relational Mission Statement:

1. What is it that you want to accomplish over the next five years?
2. My ideal spouse is like?
3. My career will look like?
4. My home will be one of (values, morals, traditions)?
5. In this statement simple is better. This is the one standing statement that you will fall back upon. It is not specifics; it is the framework for which to build your marital goals.

6. Is it practical and attainable?
7. Does the statement you set inspire you? If it does not ignite a fire for you, how will it carry you forward in your career?
8. Is your mission in line with the district vision, goals, and mission?

Sample Mission Statement:

By 2020, I will have a spouse who recognizes that we both put our relationship above all else. One who is empathetic listens and values me. I will have a career as an artist that is fulfilling to me emotional and spiritually and a home that has traditions based around family and faith first.

Do not Sacrifice Your Values for ANYBODY:

If you have to sacrifice your values, your personality, or important aspects of you to keep a relationship going this is a significant problem. The goal of a partnership is to make both of you better together. Losing a part of yourself, resentment, or not standing up for what you believe in means destroying a part of yourself to try to fit into a relationship.

Let us imagine you go to your local shoe store and find the perfect pair of shoes for you. As you shuffle through the boxes, you finally find the right ones. You open the box and try to put them on and think, "Way too tight!" You shuffle through the several other pairs of shoes, opening each like a birthday gift and hoping that these will be the same pair in your size…no luck!

You imagine that you are going to wear these shoes to every party. They are perfect in every way; except one…their size. You have dreams though, and so you continue to try to fit your foot into that shoe. Your foot hurts, blisters appear, you scream in pain as you continue to try, in vein, to make these shoes fit. You sacrifice pain and try to convince yourself that your foot (or the shoe) is the wrong size and one will change.

Unfortunately, you cannot make a shoe bigger nor your foot smaller. In a relationship, likewise, you cannot change inherently what and whom you are to "fit into" a relationship without it ending in pain and resentment. Maybe next week, maybe next year, but those feelings will rear their ugly heads at some point in the relational framework if you ignore them.

Lesson 6- Just Because You Can Drive a Car in A Videogame Does Not Mean You Have a License for the Real Thing:

"The most exciting breakthroughs of the 21st century will not occur because of technology but because of an expanding concept of what it means to be human."

--John Naisbitt

My son loves to play videogames. He plays racing games in which he has the very realistic experience of driving an exotic vehicle 200 mph. He plays games in which he simulates being an F-16 pilot, or the astronaut of an interstellar spacecraft.

Just because he has these abilities and aptitudes in a simulation game, does it necessarily mean he can do any of these things in real life? I would highly doubt that if he were given the controls of a vehicle that he was not accustomed to, or an F-16 for that matter, he would think he could succeed in piloting one of these without years of specialized training.

Yet, many of us simulate relationships through chat rooms and in social media, develop what we believe are whole relationships based on these interactions, and don't realize that they are preparation or simulations for us to play the real-world game of relational life.

On-Line... The New Hook for Relationships?

According to website, E-Harmony, 40% of the general population is now turning to on-line dating in roughly equal numbers of men and women. 20% of current committed relationships are indicated, as per this popular dating site are thanks to both partners meeting on-line.[6] According to the Pew Center, 5% of marriages now are attributed to the internet[7].

The Social Media Fables:

Many of us who post on social media are master film editors. We take pictures of the more exciting parts of our life, or, we splice out the less exhilarating aspects to paint our existence in a manner that makes us seem to lead the excitement of a reality show star.

Yet, we know the truth. How many people actually want to see that you made angel hair pasta over pesto tonight? Or that you went to gym and did your local yoga and pilates combination? Then finally came home and watched the DVR library of the television junk food that is known as reality TV?

The only reality in your self-made television miniseries that you post on social media is that you are trying to embellish your life. What is wrong with this on the surface? Nothing, however, if someone is trying to get to know you are they really getting to know the real you via the internet?

---

6 *Dating Sites Reviews*. N.p., n.d. Web. 01 May 2017.
[7] Smith, Aaron, and Monica Anderson. "5 Facts about Online Dating." Pew Research Center. N.p., 29 Feb. 2016. Web. 01 May 2017.

Probably not, it is akin to the polished, air brushed and computer generated images of a model that have been plastered on a glamour magazine cover. The picture has some truth in it, however, a majority of the photograph is so manipulated that it is difficult to say its staging to be a true representation of the person (model) themselves.

So it becomes with dating and social media profiles. Some are so airbrushed and whitewashed that they simply are not an accurate representation of the person who produced them. This leads to initiating the joining of two people on sketchy grounds of trust at some very basic levels.

The Grass Is Always Greener In The World of The Web:

The World Wide Web is a very strange place indeed. It is a place of false marketing, fake news, combined with the glitz and glamour of the Las Vegas Strip. It is a world that you can literally go to without leaving your home.

The internet can be a world without bills, deadlines, screaming children, or stress. It can be a world where everyone's life seems amazing and better than your own. People leave their banal and trivial matters on the editing floor of life and only strive to seem interesting to those in the internet domain.

The web is not the "real world," composed of so many great experiences concurrent with the day-to-day drudge of work, bills, and pressure. This means that web relationships that are devoid of all those stressors may seem like "it is quite greener" then your current brown and spotty lawn of relationships. Just know it is not always, what it appears. Read the fine print of relationships before you decide to seek greener pastures.

Not All On-Line Dating Services Are The Same:

Some on-line dating services use actual evidence-based personality screening and relationship testing. These are assessments that have been based on long-term psychological and scientific studies. Hence, they have validity that will help cut through some of the emotional aspects that fog the rational as well as, unsexy aspects of dating and finding the right mate. Of course, there is a cost to most of these services.

Remember also tha,t although you may find relationships on social media sites, which is not the main purpose. This means that those that you meet are not screened and their primary purpose may (or may not be) relationships. Additionally, how they portray themselves on these sites are not monitored which requires additional caution.

A Profile Is Your Resume and Calling Card:

When you are applying for a job you may spend hours agonizing over your resume'. Does my resume' have the right font? Does it have the right content? How do I account for job gaps? Perhaps the reason you struggle is that you know this is the only way to get your foot into the company's career door.

A parallel to this is with your dating profile, this is your resume for setting up your first interview for possible dating. If it what you say is not catchy or interesting you are likely to be swiped away via a technological device quicker than a leaf in a hurricane. If the profile is your dating resume it should be your chance to be both honest and separate yourself out from the rest of the crowd.

Remember that relational mission statement we spoke about earlier in the book? Well that should be in there in the profile. Include what you DO want in a relationship, not what you DO NOT want.

A Word About Safety:

When you open your life to the internet, you are opening a door to an exciting and intriguing world. You are also opening a chasm to a host of people that you do not know. Be certain that those that you meet have gone through some type of screening process.

As you may already know, the internet can be a great tool or a wild unchartered territory. Just make sure you take cautious steps and are as "street smart" in the virtual world as you would be in the real one. Listen to "your gut" and instincts if something seems wrong…it probably is. Do not respond to anything or anyone that asks for personal information.

Even something as innocuous as downloading something that seems like an update or new program you must be cautious. Inadvertently you may download spyware or viruses on your computer that compromises that confidential information you store in your device. If you are not certain if something is real…do not download it. If you didn't request information don't provide it. Always better to be safe than sorry in the digital realm.

Issues of cyber-bullying and cyber-stalking have been increasing in numbers exponentially. According to the website, The Guardian, cyber-stalking is now more common than physical harassment[8]. Most frighteningly, many targets are finding themselves pursued by complete strangers online.

The One BIG Thing That Is Missing In the Internet World of Relationships:

According to University of California, Professor Albert Mehrabian, verbal communication is only 7 percent verbal and 93 percent non-verbal. The non-verbal portion is composed of body language (55 percent) and tone of voice (38 percent)[9].

If this is the case, the written communication that you have with your likely spouse is, at best, verbally 7 percent. In other words, you are missing well over 93 percent of relationships cues if you are not in the room with the person. This leaves an awful lot of communication and dialogue up for grabs as to what the other person is stating in their texts and chats to you.

To assure relational success means relationships have to be conducted face to face, heart to heart, and not laptop to laptop, or smartphone to smartphone. Case and point, is the subject of so-called "Catfishing." If you are not aware of "Catfishing," it is when a person from anywhere in the world make up a factious profile and then sets out to feign a relationship with an unsuspecting victim.

---

[8] Gough, Laurie. "What It's like to Be Cyberstalked: When You Can't Escape the Untraceable Threat." The Guardian. Guardian News and Media, 07 Sept. 2016. Web. 01 May 2017.
[9] Mehrabian, Albert. "Attitudes Inferred from Non-immediacy of Verbal Communications. "Journal of Verbal Learning and Verbal Behavior 6.2 (1967): 294-95. Web.

The person becomes enthralled with this "fake profile" proceeds to send the person photos, materials, or (usually) money via a money order to some distant corner of the world. The person is eventually shocked to find out that the whole thing was a ruse. The person they "loved" never existed but was the poorly executed fabrication of a scam artist.

The victim will usually say, "How could I have been so stupid?" It is quite simple really, the person filled in the blanks and the unanswered skepticism of the victim's mind with what they want to hear. Rather then be able to judge the majority of nonverbal communications that make an interaction; it was much simpler to feel that vacuum with hopes, dreams and aspirations versus hard and real facts that may be hard to accept in the realm of loneliness.

Emotions, However, ARE Real:

Emotions are not logical or rational, so if we follow our heart and emotions we cannot always control our feelings. If you are on the internet with another person, the emotions that you may feel may be no less real to you then if you are together with each other every day. Since this is the case, try your best to protect your heart from being truly broken and be cautious when opening up.

The internet can quickly turn against you in a tidal wave of viral negativity. Private conversations and pictures can crash upon the virtual shore for everyone to pick up. Like the person throwing the millions of dying starfish back into the ocean, you simply won't be able to throw them all back in before they are viewed by the eyes of thousands of others.

In fact, Dr. Paul Zack, a professor at Claremont Graduate University, has done several studies to see how one's brain interprets relationships on-line versus in-person. His findings? The brain of the person in the relationship does not make any distinctions between the two relationships[10].

The Advantage of an On-Line Relationship: Practicality and Work on Communication:

There are, of course, many advantages to developing on-line relationships. First off, you have a wider ocean to cast your net. Instead of the small town that you are in, you now have the entire world (literally) at your fingertips. That means many more prospective fish from which to choose from.

Secondly, it is practical. You can now do everything from shopping to attending college on-line. It is as easy as opening up a laptop or turning on a smartphone. Easy access in a world that is becoming ever busier is ever simpler.

Finally, due to the lack of physical proximity with each other it fosters forcing verbal communications and trying to get to know each other. The physical part of the relationship is naturally is secondary and the speaking portion logically floats to the front.

---

[10] "Paul J. Zak - Claremont Graduate University Claremont Graduate University." Claremont Graduate University. N.p., n.d. Web. 01 May 2017.

Lesson 7- The Driver Is Still the Most Important Part of the Car:

"Being deeply loved by someone gives you strength, while loving someone deeply gives you courage."

--Lao Tzu

Only a few years ago, the idea of a car that drove itself was the stuff of fiction and sci-fi movies. Now, the first experimental self-driving cars have entered our roadways. The thought was that they would be safer, better, and allow the driver much needed work time in the busy commute to and from home.

These self-driving vehicles are essentially "computers on wheels." They have the latest of technology and can get the passengers from here to there. What is that you say? Are they safe? Well, they are still perfecting that technology and until they do the driver, not the computer, is the most important element of the car.

YOU Are The Single Most Important Part Of Your Relationship With Others:

We have all heard the old adage that "you must love yourself before anyone else can love you." Some forego this sage advice and go out looking for the person to complete them. The problem is that if you are not a complete enough person to realize what you have, how can you possibly seek what you want?

Put another way, if you do not know what size and shape your puzzle piece is, how do you know what the shape of the other puzzle piece you are seeking that will complete your life?

Do You Like Yourself?

When I work with children I often say this little catch phrase, "When you are sad and when you are blue...my best friend is me and your best friend is you!" I tell them that because no matter how crazy life gets they are only assured of one thing; they have a continuing and permanent relationship with themselves.

If they do not like who they are, this world is a lonely place no matter whom you are with. People with depression often describe being in a room full of people and still feeling at their most alone and vulnerable. Why? If you cannot accept yourself, running into the arms of another will not help you find it.

Understand Who You Are First:

Before you can find out what you want in a relationship, discover what you want for yourself. Sacrificing what you hunger for to the wants of someone else only leads to resentment. Do you really want a relationship now? How will that fit into your current lifestyle?

Am I asking you to be selfish? No, I am asking you to be self-centered. Self-Centered means that you recognize you must take care of yourself before you can be at your best for anyone else. A good analogy is that of the emergency plans that are rehearsed repeatedly, ad naueseam, when you get on an airplane. It starts with pointing out the exits and ends with oxygen masks dropping from the ceiling.

If you have a small child who do they tell you to put the oxygen mask first? Initially, you may be prompted to say, "I have got to save my baby...I am going to put it on him/her first!" Yet, if you think again, should you pass out due to lack of oxygen; both you and your child are not too long for this world. You must be at your best to help that child (or anyone else for that matter).

Self-centeredness means you realize that you must be at your finest to be of use to anyone else. If you are constantly distracted by the voices of despair in your own head, how are you possibly going to be able to help another or foster a relationship to its full bloom?

What If I Don't Like Who I Am?

All of us have aspects of ourselves we want to change or improve. Self-improvement is on a constant continuum, knowing you will never fully reach your potential. However, you should realize and be proud of where you are today.

If you do not like who you are or resent yourself as a person...you have work to do. YOU, not the person you are seeking to be with, but *you* must do the hard work of change. It has nothing to do with them and everything to do with you and being honest with what you want in your life.

If you cannot find what you like about yourself the bell should be ringing loudly in your head to get some professional help to get there. You do deserve the special relationship you desire but, most importantly, you are worthy of a relationship with peace and harmony with yourself.

Signs of Low Self-Esteem:

- Do you tend to not socialize… though you want to?
- Do you have trouble with accepting, or believing compliments?
- Are you a martyr…putting everyone's needs in front of your own?
- Do you have difficulty believing in yourself, your opinions or capabilities?
- Are you afraid to try anything new?
- Why shouldn't you believe you deserve a totally good and satisfying life?

You Make The Decisions In Your Relationships:

Often when we are in the process of seeking relationships with others we look to our family and friends to give us opinions. Listen to the opinions of others, try to take a "step back" and see if there is any validity to what they may be saying (especially if its criticism about a new potential relationship).

After that, ultimately it is your decision. You must decide if this person is what you are looking for. If you ask for advice don't dismiss it because it is not what you want to hear but make an informed and educated decision that involves both your heart and head.

A good manner of finding if this is the right one is if you would recommend your current relationship to those that are the closest to you. Would you put your stamp of approval on the parallel relationship if your sister, best friend, or eventual daughter had the same relationship? If not, why are you accepting it for yourself?

Are You Proud of Who You Are?

When you discuss your life, have you hitched your relational wagon to someone else's star? Are you proud of who you are, or is your life centered around who someone (such as your boyfriend or significant other) is? You should be pleased by who you are both in and outside of the relationship with your significant other. You are not an extension of that person; rather you are joined together as two unique and special people.

Are You A Stinkn' Thinker?

We all live in our own world of thoughts. A person's way of thinking is their 100% reality and all that really matters if we cannot get out of our way of thinking. Clearly, some of us think more accurately but it is common for all of us, to one extent or another to have distorted manners of thinking.

It is as if looking in one of those funhouse mirrors that makes you look wider, skinnier, or otherwise distorted. Many of us, at some point, have some level of this thinking due to our history and they can (and do) influence our relationships.

For instance:

Black and White Thinking: You only see extremes in your thinking. It is either "right or wrong, good or bad, perfect or terrible." In truth, there are other gray areas between those two extremes.

Personalization: Not everything is about us. Yet, if you look at life, we tend to think, "How does this affect me?" Unfortunately, the problem is not that you were not thought negatively about; it is simply you were just not thought about.

Blaming: If you are always pointing the finger at everyone else, you cannot learn how to solve the problem at hand.

Catastrophizing: Some of us see the glass as half full, some as half-empty. If you think of things with this manner of thinking, you see the sky falling down and shattering the glass.

Being Always Right: Some of us just cannot lose an argument. We will bring up anything past, present, or future (or fabricate information if needed). We will never admit we are wrong and will fight over the smallest issues just to prove we are 100% right.

Conclusion Jumper: If you tend to base your conclusions on little information, you fall into this category. Problem is, if you do not have all the information, your making decisions based on scarce or invalid information.

No One Knows You Better Than You:

Often times, a girlfriend/wife/significant other will say, "They should know what I want…they have been with me (fill in the blank) number of years." You are asking then for a psychic, not a life partner. No one can read your mind and if you play the game of, "Well they should know." No one knows you, or your specific needs and wants better then (drum roll please)….YOU!

If You Need Help Get It!

If obstacles prevent you from living your fullest life in every dimension get help. If your physical, emotional or mental health is suffering, it must be you to seek professional assistance and natural supports. No one can, or will, work harder, or more effectively, for you then you!

Recognize How Special You Are:

As I conclude this book, I want you to recognize something…you. This book is not about the other person…it is about YOU. It is about you finding what you deserve in all your relationships, including the one you carry on with yourself.

This book is about your finding your way and recognizing you deserve the very best that someone else has to offer. It is about you not allowing to sell yourself short just to be a part of a partnership or to fall in love with the word "love or marriage." It is about being honest that you deserve the hard fought and amazing byproduct of a relationship, that of true love and a lasting marriage/relationship.

Do not settle…do not give up…and do not sell yourself short. You deserve the 90+% that a committed relationship can garner for you. Making a vow is not something you should take lightly…find the right one and hold on for a wonderful, though sometimes bumpy, happy lifetime together.

About the Author:

Brett Novick lives in Ocean County, New Jersey with his wife of over twenty years, Darla, and his two children Billy and Samantha.

Professionally, Mr. Novick is a School Social Worker & Counselor and adjunct instructor at Rutgers University in New Brunswick, New Jersey.

Mr. Novick has also authored numerous articles in national and international publications ranging from family therapy, to parenting a child with autism, to educational leadership.

Mr. Novick has authored three books *Parents and Teachers Working Together* and the *Likeable, Effective, and Productive Educator, The Balanced Child: Teaching Children Social Skills & Character Building*. Additionally he wrote the children's book *Brain Bully: A Children's Guide to Stinkin' Thinkin'* published by Childswork/Childsplay and a companion game by the same title to be published in early 2018.

www.ingramcontent.com/pod-product-compliance
Lightning Source LLC
Chambersburg PA
CBHW072152020426
42334CB00018B/1967